With love

To

From

For My Love

new seasons™

a division of Publications International, Ltd.

Photo credits:
Bridgeman Art Library, London/New York: *Sunrise, Brent at Low Water* by Julian Novorol,
Private Collection; **Sharon Broutzas**; **SuperStock**: The Grand Design, Leeds;
Pushkin Museum of Fine Arts, Moscow.

Additional photography by **Sacco Productions Limited/Chicago**.

Louis Weber, CEO
Publications International, Ltd.
7373 North Cicero Avenue
Lincolnwood, Illinois 60712

Permission is never granted for commercial purposes.

Manufactured in China.

8 7 6 5 4 3 2 1

ISBN: 0-7853-6407-2

new seasons™
a division of Publications International, Ltd.

Celebrate love. It is the breath of your existence
and the best of all reasons for living.

Love makes you complete inside. A balance is achieved from two viewpoints, two backgrounds, two hearts.

*Dreams and ambitions
take hold more quickly
when you share them
with someone you love.*

Someone to lean on,
someone to laugh with,
someone to share with.
That's what love means to me.

Life's greatest treasures
lie in the hearts
of those we love.

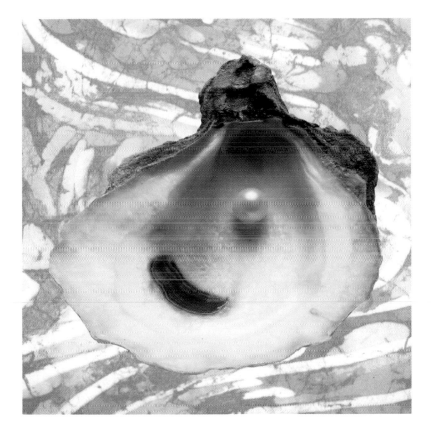

Cherish your love as you would your greatest treasure, for that is exactly what it is.

*Love is not eyes
meeting eyes across
a crowded room
but soul meeting soul
across the vastness of
space and time.*

Love around us,
love within us,
love compelling us,
love igniting us.

*Your true love is someone who loves and supports
you as you pursue your dreams.*

The path of love can take unexpected turns. But it is in its twists and turns, its hills and valleys, that we experience new and surprising joys.

Together we share each burden and multiply each joy.

When you smile,
my love, I feel joy
in my heart.

I carry my sweetheart's love with
me always, like a precious
keepsake clutched to my heart.

There is no instruction
manual for how to love.
Like laughter,
it comes naturally.

Your happiness means the world to me.

Your smile calls on me to smile.

Your laughter makes me laugh.

Playing together,
Staying together,
Eating together,
Meeting together,
Living life together,
Loving each other.

Love provides the antidote that
cures whatever ails us.

Love makes reaching milestones
more meaningful.

Your true love is someone
who listens to your dreams,
challenges your fears,
cares for your feelings,
and forgives your
shortcomings.

Create opportunities to express
your love and appreciation
to your beloved on a
regular basis.

Any dream you can dream,
Any plan you can create,
Is possible.
It all begins
With love.

The sun shines brighter when I'm in your
company. Dark clouds float away.

The road stretches out across the horizon.
Adventures lie before the two of us that
I would never undertake alone.

Traveling down unknown paths and investigating exotic opportunities is much more wonderful when someone you love joins you.

There isn't a valley steep enough

that my love can't carry me through.

Love is the closest thing
to heaven that we carry
with us every day.

If you have something to do,

someone to love,

and something to hope for,

every day becomes a celebration.

Seek out those things that make your soul sing.

Love finds us all, one way or another. Love gives us, everyone,
a reason to live and to hope. Love wraps its wings around
our weakness and carries us all the way home.

Riding on the wings of love, you can see your life from a distance and let go of the small and unimportant concerns that hold you down.

Love, like a river
on its way
to the sea,
is fed and
joined by small
streams of passion
and devotion so
that it grows
fuller and stronger
on the way.

To find joy and fulfillment, it is only necessary to trust your heart.

Your true love willingly
receives and

carefully treasures the keys
to your heart.

It is so comforting to walk into a room and
have someone understand my silence.

You are the sun and I the moon.
I am the sea to your shore.
In your arms I've finally found
the love I was searching for.

In your company, the world takes on more wonder.

*Your true love is your
favorite friend . . .*

*someone you
hear even
when they're
not around.*

Whatever our souls are made of,
his and mine are the same.

EMILY BRONTË, *WUTHERING HEIGHTS*

There is something invigorating
about new love,
with your heart pounding
every time your love draws near.
The sound of your beloved's voice
and the echo of their footsteps
are the loveliest timbre you know.

Love is contagious! If allowed to spread,
it can infect the universe with joy.

True happiness is waking each day knowing I am loved.

How do I love thee?
Let me count the ways.
I love thee to the depth and
breadth and height
My soul can reach...
I love thee with the breath,
Smiles, tears, of all my life!—
and, if God choose,
I shall but love thee better
after death.

ELIZABETH BARRETT BROWNING,
SONNETS FROM THE PORTUGUESE

The miracle of love may begin with a simple smile.

*There are not enough flowers, candy boxes, or candlelit dinners
to equal the sheer romantic power of one privately shared joke
between a loving couple.*

*My love, you can
see into my heart.*

Love leads us on a path
of happiness through life.

I have my shoulders
to carry my burdens,
a creative mind to figure out solutions,
and a strong heart to weather disappointment.
But I have yet one more tool to successfully face
anything this world can throw my way:
I have you.

*Love is not a
protective cage,
but the gift of
wings that sets
me free.*

When we believe in each other, we act as angels, sharing our confidence and the power of our faith. It is no small thing to look into your loved one's eyes, straight and true, and to say with sincerity, "I believe in you."

Lovers share the same vision, but through different sets of eyes.

*Love is not just the touching
of two hearts, it is the
blending of two lives.*

Come walk with me
through life, my love,
arm in arm we'll stroll.
With love and hope
to light our path
and faith to guide our souls.

When I am plodding through my day,
thoroughly immersed in life's present drama,
love opens my eyes to pleasant events,
happy endings, and hidden treasures.

Show me a heart without love, and I'll show you
a life that has yet to be blessed.

There is no remedy for love but to love more.

HENRY DAVID THOREAU

A love like ours doesn't happen every day.
I'm glad you happened to me.